TOTALITY!

An Eclipse Guide in Rhyme and Science

Jeffrey Bennett

BIG KID SCIENCE

Design and Production: Mark Stuart Ong, Susan Riley, Side By Side Studios

Published in the United States by
Big Kid Science
Boulder, Colorado
www.BigKidScience.com

ISBN: 978-1-937548-90-2
[ebook: 978-1-937548-91-9]
Printed and bound in China by RR Donnelley APS

Also by Jeffrey Bennett

For children
> *Max Goes to the Moon*
> *Max Goes to Mars*
> *Max Goes to Jupiter*
> *Max Goes to the Space Station*
> *The Wizard Who Saved the World*
> *I, Humanity*

For grownups
> *Beyond UFOs*
> *Math for Life*
> *What Is Relativity?*
> *On Teaching Science*
> *A Global Warming Primer*

Textbooks
> *The Cosmic Perspective*
> *The Essential Cosmic Perspective*
> *The Cosmic Perspective Fundamentals*
> *Life in the Universe*
> *Using and Understanding Mathematics*
> *Statistical Reasoning for Everyday Life*

Illustration Credits
Cover: Miloslav Druckmüller
p. 3. App photo: Miloslav Druckmüller
p. 4. Michael Zeiler, GreatAmericanEclipse.com, based on eclipse code by Xavier Jubier
p. 6. Rick Fienberg, TravelQuest International, and Wilderness Travel
p. 7. Based on eclipse predictions by Fred Espenak, NASA GSFC.
p. 9. Château de Courcelles
p. 10. Wikimedia Commons/ Bruno Girin
p. 13. Alan Okamoto (from *Max Goes to the Moon*)
pp. 14–16: Michael Carroll, adapted from Bennett, Donahue, Schneider, and Voit, *The Cosmic Perspective*, 9th Edition (2020), with permission of Pearson Education, Upper Saddle River, NJ.

p. 17. total, partial photos: Giuseppe Donatiello; penumbral: Wikimedia Commons/ Tomruen
p. 18 (photos). Rick Fienberg, TravelQuest International, and Wilderness Travel
p. 19. Xavier Jubier
p. 20. NASA/DSCOVR
pp. 21, 22. From the *Totality* app, eclipse code by Xavier Jubier
p. 23. Clara Johnson
p. 24. Chuck and Susan Rheule
p. 25. Miloslav Druckmüller
p. 26. Mike Simmons
p. 27. NASA/ Aubrey Gemignani

All other artwork created by Mark Stuart Ong, for Big Kid Science.

Expert Reviewers
Leilani Arthurs, University of Colorado
Courtney Black, ISS National Lab
Noella Dcruz, Joliet Junior College
Megan Donahue, Michigan State University
Xinnan Du, Kavli Institute, Stanford University
Doug Duncan, University of Colorado
Erica Ellingson, University of Colorado
Rick Fienberg, American Astronomical Society
Donna Governor, University of North Georgia
Sarah Haisley, Ivy Tech Community College
Kelsey Johnson, University of Virginia
Ichshiro Konno, University of Texas, San Antonio
Larry Lebofsky, Planetary Science Institute
Mark Levy, Brooklyn College
Larry Morris, aka "Professor Boggs"
James Negus, University of Colorado
Nick Schneider, University of Colorado
Seth Shostak, SETI Institute
Mike Simmons, Blue Marble Space Institute
Patricia Tribe, Story Time From Space
Helen Zentner, Brooklyn College

Special thanks for great suggestions on the rhyme: Larry Morris, Cara Falcetti, Megan Donahue, James Negus, Leilani Arthurs, Seth Shostak, Wendy Crumrine, Brooke Bennett

Classroom Reviewers
And with great appreciation to the following teachers for testing this book with their students: Heather Bunting (Shore Preparatory, North Sydney, Australia), Cara Falcetti (Manhattan Day School, NY), Mare Gilmore (Silver Sands School, Okaloosa County, FL), Kaci Heins (Shelby West Middle, Shelbyville, KY), Alex Hibert (Central Elementary, Longmont, CO), Holli Hoskins (Foothill Elementary, Boulder, CO), Emily Kathryn Vazquez Archer (Virginia Academy), Jonathan Warshaw (Foothill Elementary, Boulder, CO), Sara Wrightstone (Harrisburg Catholic Elementary, PA)

Dedication

A total solar eclipse is among the most awe-inspiring events in nature, but relatively few people have had the opportunity to experience one. This book is dedicated to helping to change that. I also hope it will help readers appreciate the value of science, which not only makes it possible to explain and predict eclipses but can also help us build a more peaceful, fair, and sustainable future for ourselves and generations to come.

And to my parents, for always encouraging me to be curious and to follow the evidence as we seek to uncover truth.

The *Totality* App

This book is designed to be used along with the free app *Totality by Big Kid Science*, which you can download from the iOS or Android app stores or through BigKidScience.com/eclipse.

A Note from the Author

The title and focus of this book puts emphasis on the incredible experience of seeing a total solar eclipse, and the map on page 7 shows you where you can view totality through 2045. But keep in mind that all eclipses are worth viewing, including partial and annular solar eclipses and lunar eclipses, and many web sites can help you learn when and where these "other" types of eclipses will be visible. (The Totality app Learn screen also includes a link that lists other future eclipses.)

So whether or not you are able to experience totality in the near future, I hope you will take the opportunity to view all types of eclipses – and that this book will help you both to understand the amazing natural phenomena that you are witnessing and to appreciate the scientific achievements that make eclipse prediction possible.

Enjoy the view!

Jeffrey Bennett

Imagine that you've made all your plans carefully, and today is the day you will see the Moon block out the Sun in a total solar eclipse. This book offers a short rhyme designed to help you understand and remember what you'll experience, accompanied by illustrations and "Big Kid Boxes" that discuss the underlying science.

To get the most out of this book:

- First, read through the rhyme while trying to guess at the underlying science that it describes.
- Next, study the illustrations and read the Big Kid Boxes, thinking carefully about how the rhyme and science connect.
- Finally, confirm your understanding with the help of the Glossary, Activities, and Summary at the end of the book.

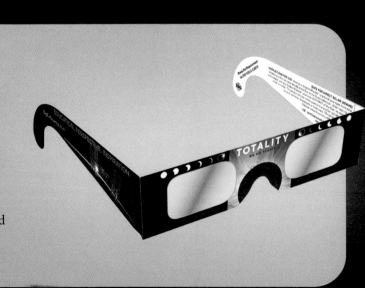

Eclipse Glasses

Warning: *Except **during** totality, it is never safe to look directly at the Sun unless you are wearing your special eclipse glasses.*

The best way to enjoy a solar eclipse is by using special eclipse glasses; see page 24 for details on their use. (Do not use ordinary sunglasses; they are not safe!) Be sure that your glasses meet the ISO 12312-2 international standard, and purchase only from a reputable vendor such as the Totality app shop (bigkidscience.com/eclipse/shop) or others on the reputable vendor list at eclipse.aas.org.

Note that you don't have to wait for an eclipse to use them. As long as they are undamaged and fully shield your eyes, you can safely use eclipse glasses to view the Sun at any time. If you have good eyesight, the glasses may even allow you to see a few sunspots.

Today's the day, it's finally come
I'll see a diamond on the Sun

This photo shows the "diamond ring effect," which lasts only a second or so just before and after totality.

What makes it look like a diamond ring?

The Sun is much too hot to have any solid material like diamond. But as you can see in the photo, the Sun can very briefly look like a diamond ring during a total solar eclipse.

You can understand this *diamond ring effect* by knowing that the Sun has both a visible surface (called the *photosphere*) and a thin atmosphere (the *chromosphere* and *corona*, discussed on page 25) that extends high above that surface. Ordinarily, we see only the Sun's surface, because its bright light drowns out the faint light from its atmosphere. The exception occurs when the Moon completely blocks out the Sun's surface during **totality**. We see the diamond ring just before totality, as the last bit of bright light from the Sun's surface disappears, and again as sunlight re-emerges after totality. The "diamond" is that bit of bright sunlight and the "ring" is the Sun's atmosphere appearing around the edges of the Moon.

Note: The diamond ring lasts only for a second or so, and you can see it only if you have removed your eclipse glasses, which must stay on until the diamond ring begins. For this reason, it is often easier to see the second diamond ring at the end of totality (and then immediately put your glasses back on).

It happens somewhere almost every year
But rarely is that somewhere right here

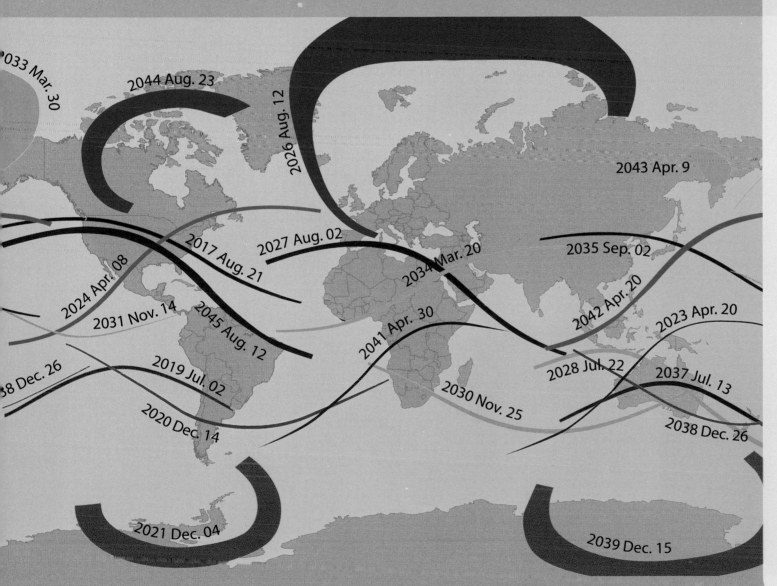

Paths of totality for all total solar eclipses from 2017 through 2045. Pairs of the same color are separated by the approximately 18-year, 11-day period known as the *saros cycle* (see page 10). *Note*: Paths in the far north and south look wider only because of the map projection; on a globe, you would see that they are just as narrow as other paths.

How often can you see a total solar eclipse?

On average, a total solar eclipse happens *somewhere* on Earth about every year and a half, but to see it you must be within the *path of totality*. The map on this page shows paths of totality for recent and upcoming total solar eclipses. The fact that the paths are quite narrow explains why eclipses are rare in any one place.

In fact, the *average* time between total solar eclipses at any particular location is about 375 years, though there can be great variations. For example, a small region south of St. Louis, Missouri (USA) had two total solar eclipses in just 7 years (2017 and 2024). In contrast, Los Angeles last had a total solar eclipse on May 22, 1724, and will not have another until April 1, 3290.

Of course, you don't have to wait for an eclipse to come to you. Many people plan trips to see these amazing events, and hopefully you'll soon be one of them!

We're talking a total eclipse of the Sun
An incredible sight, second to none!

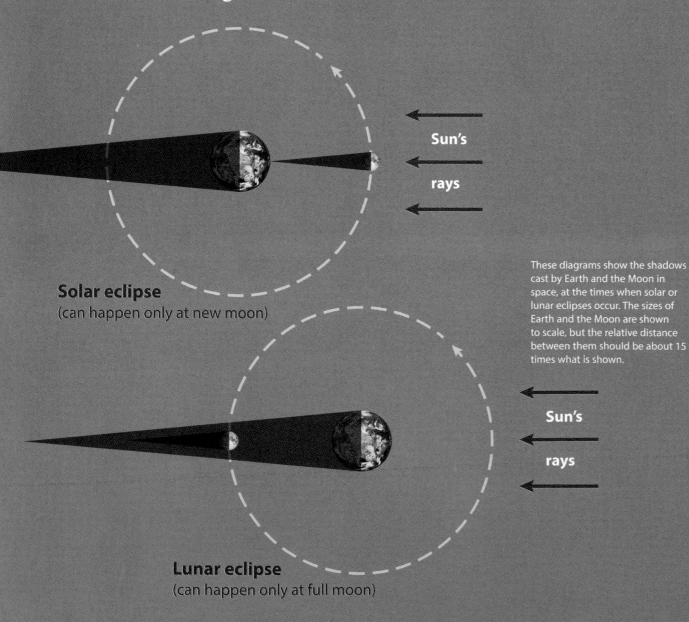

Sun's

rays

Solar eclipse
(can happen only at new moon)

These diagrams show the shadows cast by Earth and the Moon in space, at the times when solar or lunar eclipses occur. The sizes of Earth and the Moon are shown to scale, but the relative distance between them should be about 15 times what is shown.

Sun's

rays

Lunar eclipse
(can happen only at full moon)

How is a solar eclipse different from a lunar eclipse?

There are two basic types of eclipse: *solar* (meaning "of the Sun") and *lunar* (meaning "of the Moon"). This page shows the difference between them. Notice that both Earth and the Moon cast shadows pointing away from the Sun in space. A solar eclipse occurs when the Moon's shadow falls on Earth (which can happen only at new moon), and a lunar eclipse occurs when Earth's shadow falls on the Moon (which can only happen at full moon).

Overall, solar and lunar eclipses occur about equally often. However, from any particular location, you are much more likely to see a lunar eclipse. The diagrams show why. Notice that the Moon's shadow can touch only a small portion of Earth during a solar eclipse, so only the relatively few people within that region will see a particular solar eclipse. In contrast, any lunar eclipse is visible to about half the world, because Earth's shadow on the Moon can be seen from almost anywhere on Earth's night side.

In ancient times it caused quite a fright
When people saw daytime turn into night

For a few brief moments, a total solar eclipse turns day into night, as shown in this photo taken during a 1999 eclipse over Château de Courcelles in France. (The spikes around the Sun are camera artifacts.)

How can science change fear to empowerment?

For most of human history, a solar eclipse was a source of great fear. As the Sun began to disappear in daytime, some of our ancestors imagined it as a sign of angry gods, others as celestial monsters consuming the Sun. One ancient Greek story tells of two great armies massing for battle, but becoming so frightened by an eclipse that they laid down their weapons, signed a peace treaty, and went home.

Today, you can have a very different reaction to a total solar eclipse. You can applaud when the Sun disappears at the exact moment predicted by scientists. You can look up in awe at the beautiful sight of the Sun's corona. And you can marvel at the fact that events that mystified and terrified our ancestors are now so well understood that we can predict them thousands of years in advance.

This remarkable change in the human perspective on eclipses holds an important lesson: By focusing on *science* rather than fears or myths, we not only create understanding but also empower ourselves with the knowledge needed to build a better world. Let's hope that as you grow up, we will put science to good use in helping us to overcome the challenges we now face and in creating new technologies to improve the lives of people everywhere.

Today we know it's a great cosmic dance
And predict its movements, far in advance

This photo shows the remains of an ancient Maya observatory at Chichén Itzá (Mexico).

Could ancient civilizations predict eclipses?

The rhyme refers to a "cosmic dance" because eclipses occur when Earth, Moon, and Sun (the cosmic "dancers") fall into line. Modern science allows us to predict this "dance" far in advance and in virtually perfect detail. Ancient people could not do this, because they did not yet know that Earth orbits the Sun and the Moon orbits Earth as described by the law of gravity.

Nevertheless, by keeping careful records of astronomical events over many generations, a few ancient civilizations (including the Babylonians, Chinese, and Maya) discovered an important fact about the *timing* of eclipses: Eclipses follow a pattern that repeats about every 18 years, 11 days. You can *see* this time period, called the **saros cycle**, on the map on page 7. Notice, for example, that the total solar eclipse of September 2, 2035, comes 18 years, 11 days after the solar eclipse of August 21, 2017.

This ancient achievement holds another important lesson about science. Namely, that science progresses through careful work in which each generation builds upon the work of those that have come before. As the famous scientist Isaac Newton (who discovered the law of gravity) wrote about his own work: "If I have seen further, it is by standing on the shoulders of giants."

Three dancers there are — Earth, Moon, and Sun

When they line up, the eclipse has begun

Moon

Earth

The Moon is much smaller than the Sun, but it is just the right distance from Earth to block your view of the Sun during a total solar eclipse. For this and other diagrams in this book showing Earth, Moon, and Sun: the sizes of Earth and the Moon are shown to scale, but the relative distances and the size of the Sun are all much greater than shown.

How can our small Moon block our gigantic Sun?

The Sun is about 400 times as large in diameter as the Moon, but it is also about 400 times as far away from Earth. As a result, the Moon is just the right size to block your view of the Sun during a total solar eclipse. (However, as we'll discuss on page 18, the Moon's distance from Earth varies somewhat, so it's not always a perfect fit.)

Astronomically speaking, the fact that the Moon can just barely cover the Sun (as seen from Earth) is an amazing coincidence. If the Moon were farther away from us, it would never completely block our view of the Sun's surface. If it were closer, it would block part of the Sun's atmosphere as well as the surface, making eclipses less spectacular.

We are lucky to live at a time when this coincidence exists, because the Moon is very gradually moving farther away from Earth (by only about 3.8 centimeters, or 1½ inches, per year!). Many millions of years ago, when the Moon was closer to Earth, it *did* cover the Sun's atmosphere during eclipses. And about a billion years from now, the Moon will have moved far enough away that total solar eclipses will no longer occur.

This idea will become much more clear
Knowing Earth orbits Sun, once each year

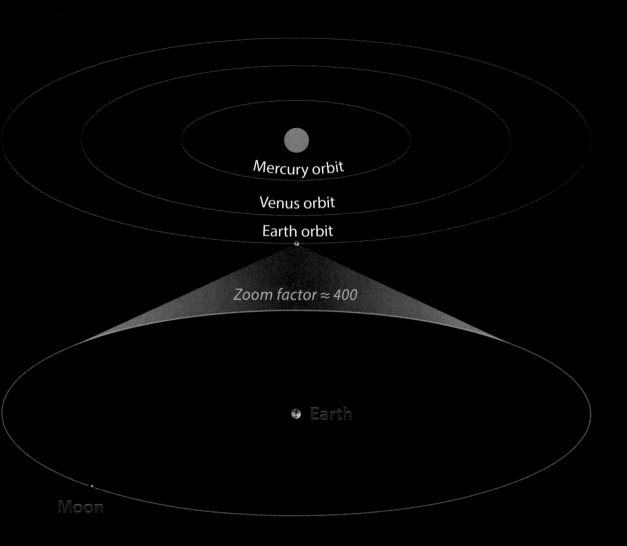

Mercury orbit

Venus orbit

Earth orbit

Zoom factor ≈ 400

Earth

Moon

These diagrams show Earth's orbit around the Sun and the Moon's orbit around Earth. The "zoom factor" of 400 tells you the size difference between these orbits. (The orbits are actually nearly circular, but appear more elliptical because this diagram views them at an angle.)

How does the Moon's orbit compare to Earth's?

The rhyme on this and the next page captures two key facts needed to understand eclipses: (1) Earth orbits the Sun once each year, and (2) the Moon orbits Earth in a little less than a month. The diagrams show how the two orbits compare in size.

The big difference in orbital sizes explains why the Moon's orbit is too small to see without zooming in, which has an important effect: It means that, for practical purposes, the direction to the Sun is the same no matter whether you are looking at it from Earth or the Moon. That's why the diagram on page 8 shows rays of sunlight all coming at Earth and the Moon from a single direction, and why there's only a single "to Sun" arrow in the diagram on the next page.

Keep in mind that although the diagrams show Earth and the Moon in one place, in reality they are constantly moving along their orbits. It is the combination of these orbital motions that leads to the Moon's cycle of phases (from new moon to new moon or full moon to full moon) taking about 29½ days. You'll notice that this is approximately a month, and that's *not* a coincidence. Our word *month* (think "moonth") comes from the Moon's 29½-day cycle of phases.

While Moon orbits Earth, showing phase after phase
Repeating each twenty-nine and one-half days

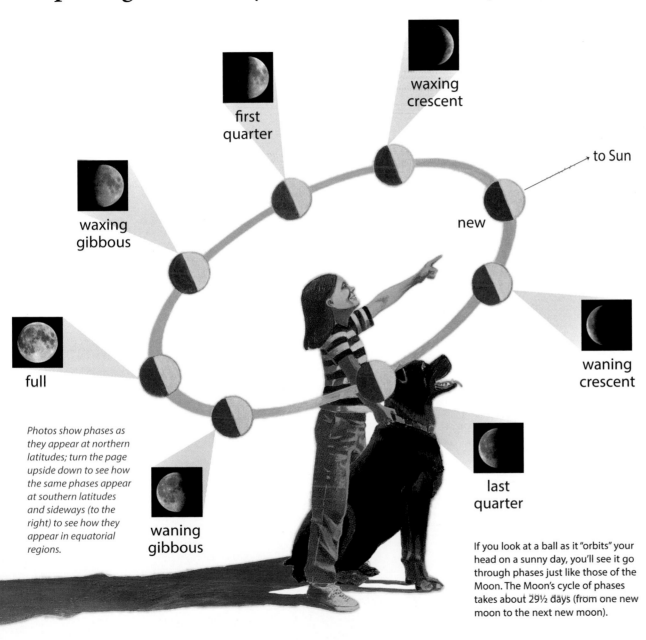

first quarter

waxing crescent

waxing gibbous

to Sun

new

full

waning crescent

Photos show phases as they appear at northern latitudes; turn the page upside down to see how the same phases appear at southern latitudes and sideways (to the right) to see how they appear in equatorial regions.

waning gibbous

last quarter

If you look at a ball as it "orbits" your head on a sunny day, you'll see it go through phases just like those of the Moon. The Moon's cycle of phases takes about 29½ days (from one new moon to the next new moon).

Why do we see phases of the Moon?

You can understand Moon *phases* with a simple demonstration: Take a ball outside on a sunny day and hold it at arm's length as you spin counterclockwise. You'll see the ball go through phases just like the Moon. The diagram shows why. Notice that half of the ball (or Moon) always faces the Sun while the other half faces away. However, from your vantage point in the middle, you will see the ball (or Moon) in different phases at different points in its orbit, because you will be viewing different portions of its sunlit and dark sides. For example, in the *first quarter* position, you will see equal amounts of the sunlit and dark sides, so the ball (or Moon) will appear to be half bright and half dark.

For eclipses, the important phases are new and full, because these are the only phases at which our "cosmic dancers" (Earth, Moon, and Sun) can fall into a perfect line. A solar eclipse can occur only at new moon, when the Moon lies in the same direction as the Sun in the sky. A lunar eclipse can occur only at full moon, when the Moon is directly opposite the Sun in the sky.

Indeed, if you look only at the diagrams we've shown so far, you might wonder why we don't see an eclipse at *every* new and full moon. The answer comes from details of the orbits, which we will begin to explore on the next page.

These orbits are tilted, which helps to explain
Why eclipses do not form a monthly refrain

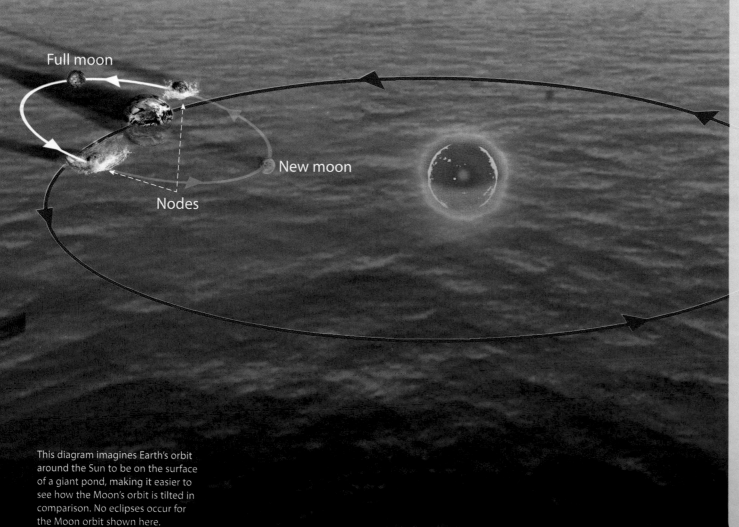

Full moon

New moon

Nodes

This diagram imagines Earth's orbit around the Sun to be on the surface of a giant pond, making it easier to see how the Moon's orbit is tilted in comparison. No eclipses occur for the Moon orbit shown here.

Why isn't there an eclipse at every new and full moon?

The reason that eclipses do not occur at *every* new and full moon (that is, they "do not form a monthly refrain") is simple: It is because the Moon's orbit around Earth is tilted (by about 5°) compared to Earth's orbit around the Sun.

You can visualize this idea by imagining that Earth orbits the Sun on the surface of a giant pond.* The tilt of the Moon's orbit then means that the Moon spends most of its time either above or below the pond surface, "splashing through" only at two points, called *nodes*, during each orbit.

Notice that, for the Moon orbit shown on this page, the new moon's shadow passes below Earth and Earth's shadow passes below the full moon. As a result, we do *not* have eclipses at these times.

*More technically, the pond surface represents the plane of Earth's orbit around the Sun, called the *ecliptic plane*, so the nodes are the points where the Moon's orbit crosses through the ecliptic plane.

An eclipse of the Sun can only arise
when new moon and two orbits all coincide

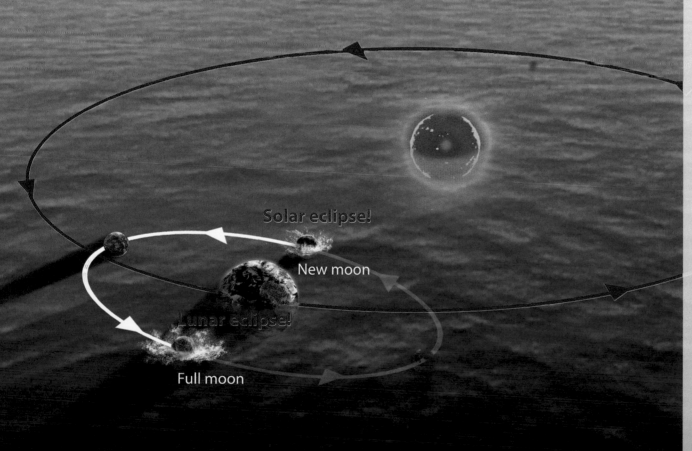

Solar eclipse!

New moon

Lunar eclipse!

Full moon

We see the "Moon pond" again, but this time with the Moon's orbit at a position where eclipses *do* occur.

What conditions allow for an eclipse?

This page repeats the "Moon pond" from the prior page, except with Earth (along with the Moon's orbit) in a different position in its orbit around the Sun. Notice that new moon and full moon now occur *at* the nodes (the splashes) of the Moon's orbit. As a result, the Moon's shadow falls directly on Earth at new moon, causing a solar eclipse, and Earth's shadow falls on the Moon at full moon, causing a lunar eclipse.

To summarize, there are two basic conditions for any eclipse:

1. the phase of the Moon must be either new (for a solar eclipse) or full (for a lunar eclipse), and
2. the new or full moon must occur at a time when the nodes are aligned (or almost aligned) with Earth and the Sun.

Remembering that the nodes are the points in the Moon's orbit around Earth that cross through the plane of Earth's orbit around the Sun, you can see why the rhyme summarizes the conditions for a solar eclipse by saying that "new moon and two orbits all coincide."

Challenge Question: Can you identify any other places in the Moon pond illustration where eclipses will also occur?

15

This happens just about twice every year
At each of those times, an eclipse will appear

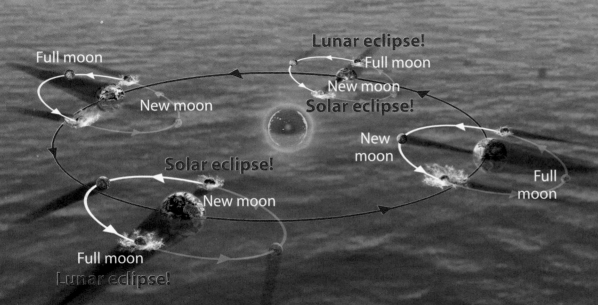

Full moon

New moon

Lunar eclipse!
Full moon
New moon
Solar eclipse!

New moon

Full moon

Solar eclipse!
New moon

Full moon
Lunar eclipse!

Now we see the "Moon pond" with Earth and the Moon's orbit in four positions, two of which have a solar eclipse at new moon and a lunar eclipse at full moon.

Why do eclipses happen about twice each year?

If you successfully answered the challenge question on the prior page, you'll recognize that this page shows the *two* places (lower left and upper right) on the "Moon pond" where new and full moons occur close enough to nodes (splashes) to allow for eclipses. Because the big orbit in the diagram represents Earth's year-long orbit around the Sun, we conclude that eclipses can occur during two time periods each year. Each of these periods, called *eclipse seasons*, last about 5 weeks.

In fact, we *always* have some type of solar eclipse and some type of lunar eclipse during each eclipse season, though the eclipses are not always total. That is why, in continuing to focus on an eclipse of the Sun, the rhyme tells us that such an eclipse happens about "twice every year."

Advanced Note: You might wonder why the rhyme says that a solar eclipse happens *about* (rather than exactly) twice each year. The answer (not shown in this diagram) is that the Moon's entire orbit slowly turns, or *precesses*, in a way that gradually changes the positions of the nodes, so that eclipse seasons occur only about 173 days apart (which is less than 6 months). It is this fact that leads to eclipses repeating in the approximately 18-year, 11-day saros cycle rather than repeating exactly twice each year.

But only for those who are in the right place
And it's not always total, 'cause we're dealing with space

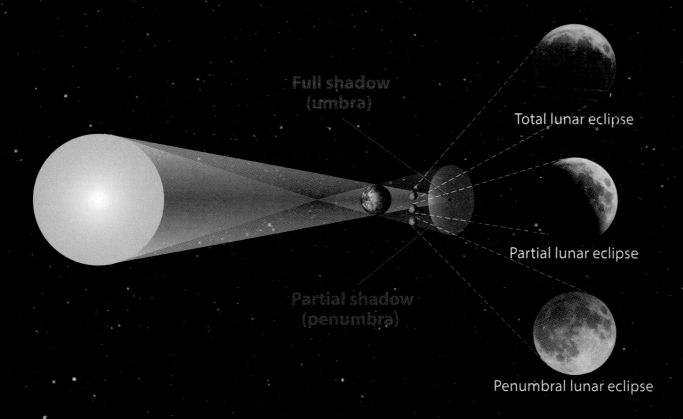

Full shadow
(umbra)

Total lunar eclipse

Partial lunar eclipse

Partial shadow
(penumbra)

Penumbral lunar eclipse

An eclipse shadow has two regions: full and partial. This diagram shows how this fact leads to three types of lunar eclipse. The reddish color of a total lunar eclipse comes from light that is bent by Earth's atmosphere toward the Moon.

How do eclipse shadows lead to three types of lunar eclipse?

So far, the illustrations in this book have shown eclipse shadows as simple cones. However, "we're dealing with space," and the Sun's large size means that an eclipse shadow actually has two regions: a *full shadow* (also called the *umbra*) in which sunlight is fully blocked, and a *partial shadow* (or *penumbra*) in which sunlight is only partially blocked.

The diagram on this page shows Earth's shadow regions and the three types of lunar eclipse that can occur as a result. We see a *total lunar eclipse* when the Moon is completely within the full shadow, a *partial lunar eclipse* when it is only partially in the full shadow, and a *penumbral lunar eclipse* (in which the full moon appears only slightly dimmer than normal) when it is within just the partial shadow.

Be sure to note: The obvious curvature of Earth's full shadow during a partial lunar eclipse provides absolute proof that our world is round (spherical), because no other planet shape could lead to a round shadow in all lunar eclipses. Indeed, this fact helped the ancient Greeks recognize that Earth must be round more than two thousand years ago.

If the Moon is off center, or slightly too far
Your eclipse will be partial or just an-nu-lar

A total solar eclipse occurs where the Moon's full shadow touches the Earth.

Sun

Moon

Earth

The Moon appears "off center" within the partial shadow, creating a partial solar eclipse.

Sometimes, a solar eclipse happens when the Moon is "too far" away, so its full shadow does not reach the Earth . . .

Sun

Moon

Earth

. . . creating an annular eclipse behind the full shadow (and partial solar eclipse in the partial shadow).

The Moon's varying distance from Earth affects solar eclipses. When the Moon is relatively close to Earth (top), we can get a total solar eclipse. When the Moon is relatively far (bottom), we get an annular eclipse. In either case, a partial solar eclipse occurs in regions touched by the Moon's partial shadow.

Total solar eclipse

Partial solar eclipse

Annular eclipse

What are the three types of solar eclipse?

We've now switched the positions of Earth and the Moon (compared to page 17) to show the three types of *solar* eclipse, for which you need one more fact: The Moon's distance from Earth varies somewhat (because its orbital shape is an ellipse rather than a perfect circle). Just as your thumb can block more of your view when it is closer to your eye, the Moon can block more of the Sun when it is closer to Earth. (Earth's distance from the Sun also varies slightly, but this effect is smaller.)

The top diagram shows what happens when the Moon is relatively close to Earth. In that case, the Moon's full shadow touches a small region of Earth, fully blocking the Sun to create a *total solar eclipse* within this region. The Moon's partial shadow covers a larger, surrounding region in which the Moon will appear "off center," creating a *partial solar eclipse*.

Now look at the lower diagram, in which the Moon is "too far" to fully block the Sun. In this case, the region behind the full shadow gets an *annular eclipse* (*annular* means "ring-shaped"), in which the Moon is encircled by a ring of sunlight (sometimes called the "ring of fire").

Warning: You must wear eclipse glasses to look at a partial or annular eclipse.

And even when all is as it should be
You must be *in* the shadow for to-tal-ity

This map shows the percentage of the Sun blocked by the Moon in different locations for the solar eclipse of April 8, 2024.

Do I really have to be *in* the path of totality?

Maps like the one on this page show the percentage of the Sun blocked at different locations during a solar eclipse. Such maps might tempt you to think that if you have, say, a 90% eclipse, you'll get 90% of the total eclipse experience. *But this is not the case.*

To understand why, imagine that you are *very* close to the path of totality — so close that that the Moon will cover 99% of the Sun. Although that's "almost" a total solar eclipse, the Sun is so bright that the remaining 1% will prevent you from seeing the most amazing parts of a total eclipse. For example, you won't see the diamond ring or the Sun's atmosphere or the sky becoming dark enough to see planets and stars. It's no exaggeration to say that in the case of a solar eclipse, the difference between total and "almost total" is the difference between night and day.

So if you want to see a total eclipse (and you do!), make sure that you get into the path of totality, not just close to it. Of course, if you simply can't get to the path of totality but are in a location that will have a partial solar eclipse, you should still watch (use your eclipse glasses!), even though it won't be nearly the same experience.

The shadow is round, and not very wide

along a thin path, it rapidly glides

This image shows the Moon's round shadow over the eastern United States during the 2017 total solar eclipse. The visible shadow includes all of the Moon's full shadow and the darker parts of its partial shadow.

How big and how fast is the shadow?

The Moon is round, so both its full and partial shadows are also round.* The sizes of the shadows during a particular eclipse depend on the Moon's distance from Earth at the time. The full shadow never covers a region more than about 270 kilometers (167 miles) across and usually is much smaller (and sometimes does not even reach Earth). The partial shadow is much larger (more than 6,000 kilometers across), which is why there is a partial solar eclipse in a wide region around the path of totality.

The shadows do not stay in one place, both because Earth rotates underneath them and because the Moon is moving in its orbit. Together, these motions cause the shadows to race across Earth's surface at a typical speed near 1,600 kilometers per hour (1,000 miles per hour). That is why totality does not last more than a few minutes in any one place.

* The shadow is round, but because it hits some parts of Earth at an angle, it may cover an area that is oval-shaped.

So if you'd like to see a total eclipse
Find a good map and plan out your trip

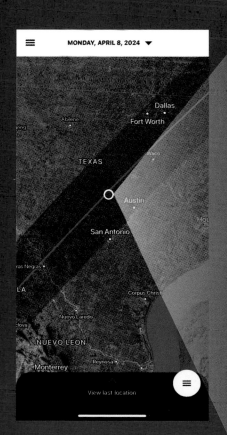

You can use the *Totality* app (and many websites) to explore the path of totality, helping you select a location for your eclipse trip. Here, we see a portion of the path near Austin (Texas) for the eclipse of April 8, 2024, along with a box telling you when and what you would see at the marked location.

Where should I go to see totality?

The first step in planning your total eclipse trip is to study a map like that on page 7 to identify a future eclipse with a path and date that works for you. Then use the *Totality* app (or an online tool) to explore the path of totality in detail. You should try to balance three things in deciding where to watch the eclipse:

1. Choose a location that you can actually get to. In most cases, this means being within a reasonable driving distance, unless you plan to fly to the eclipse path or watch the eclipse from a ship.

2. Choose a location with a good chance of clear skies during the eclipse, because you need that to get the full experience (see page 27). This requires a bit of luck since you'll plan your trip long before there's a weather forecast for eclipse day, but many eclipse websites will tell you the likelihood of clouds based on historical weather data. If the weather forecast is poor for eclipse day, consider whether you can move to a more promising location.

3. Try to get as much time in totality as possible. Totality can never last more than about 7½ minutes, and for most eclipses the maximum length is much shorter. Still, the length will vary along the path (and is longer near the centerline than the edges), and longer is better if the skies are clear.

When the day comes, the daylight will dim
For more than an hour as action begins

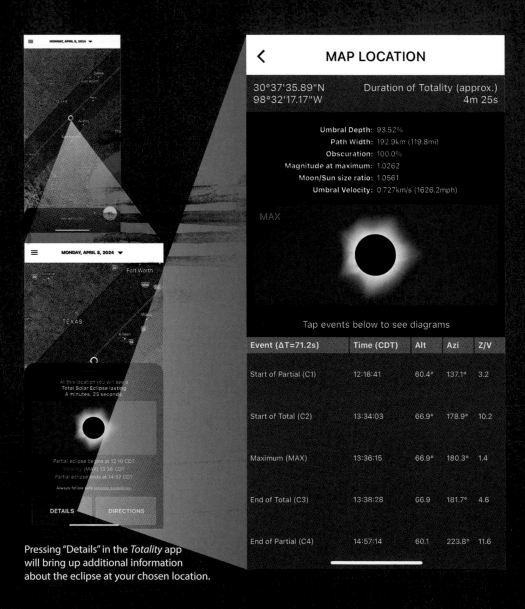

MAP LOCATION

30°37'35.89"N
98°32'17.17"W

Duration of Totality (approx.)
4m 25s

Umbral Depth: 93.52%
Path Width: 192.9km (119.8mi)
Obscuration: 100.0%
Magnitude at maximum: 1.0262
Moon/Sun size ratio: 1.0561
Umbral Velocity: 0.727km/s (1626.2mph)

MAX

Tap events below to see diagrams

Event (ΔT=71.2s)	Time (CDT)	Alt	Azi	Z/V
Start of Partial (C1)	12:16:41	60.4°	137.1°	3.2
Start of Total (C2)	13:34:03	66.9°	178.9°	10.2
Maximum (MAX)	13:36:15	66.9°	180.3°	1.4
End of Total (C3)	13:38:28	66.9	181.7°	4.6
End of Partial (C4)	14:57:14	60.1	223.8°	11.6

Pressing "Details" in the *Totality* app will bring up additional information about the eclipse at your chosen location.

What will happen on eclipse day?

The eclipse will proceed as shown in the "Details" table for your location. It begins at the moment called "Start of Partial" (also called "first contact," or "C1"), which is when the Moon first seems to touch the Sun. Over the next hour or so, the Moon will gradually appear to take a bigger and bigger bite out of the Sun until you see the diamond ring effect and the start of totality. This is the moment called "Start of Total" (or "second contact," or "C2").

Remember that totality won't last long. Its midpoint is called "Maximum" in the table, and it ends with the second diamond ring at the time called "End of Total" (or "third contact," or "C3"). You'll then be back to a partial solar eclipse, but now with the Moon gradually moving off the Sun. This second partial phase lasts until the time called "End of Partial" (or "fourth contact," or "C4"), which marks the end of the entire event.

You can understand this progression by thinking about the full (umbra) and partial (penumbra) shadows racing over the face of the Earth. You see a partial eclipse during the times when the partial shadow is over your location, and totality during the short time that the much smaller full shadow passes over you.

Animals will start to act very strange
Patterns of light will gradually change

This photo shows light shining through tree leaves onto the ground shortly before totality during a solar eclipse. The many small crescents are images of the mostly eclipsed Sun.

What will you notice as totality approaches?

The beginning of the eclipse will be barely noticeable (unless you look up at the Sun with your eclipse glasses), but the pace of the action will gradually pick up. The sky will darken more dramatically as totality approaches, and you may feel a shiver as the temperature drops. You'll notice changes in colors and lighting, including shadows becoming much sharper, as light comes from a shrinking portion of the Sun.

Trees around you will project multiple small images of the partially eclipsed Sun, because the small spaces between the tree leaves act like "pinhole cameras" (see page 24). If you are on a hilltop and have a clear horizon, you may see the Moon's full shadow racing toward you across the landscape. Sometimes, just before (and after) totality, you may see shimmering waves of light and dark, called *shadow bands*, rippling over the ground around you.

Animal behavior can be especially interesting as totality approaches. For example, birds that sing in the daytime may become silent, while owls and bats that sleep during the day may wake up. You should pay close attention, because you never know exactly what animals will do when they are confused by darkness in daytime.

You can use eclipse glasses to protect your eyes
But don't take them off 'til the moment arrives

How can I watch the eclipse safely?

It is never safe to look at the Sun's surface without protection. This means you will want special *eclipse glasses* like those that come with this book. Be sure that your eclipse glasses are undamaged, so that no dangerous sunlight can come through.

The only time that you can safely remove your eclipse glasses (while looking toward the Sun) is during totality, when the Moon completely blocks the Sun's surface. In other words, here is how you should use eclipse glasses to watch a total solar eclipse:

- During the partial phase before totality, don't look toward the Sun unless you are wearing your eclipse glasses.
- For the short period of totality, starting when the diamond ring effect begins, you *can and should* remove your eclipse glasses. Leaving the glasses on during totality would mean missing the experience. (*Don't* remove them if the eclipse is annular rather than total.)
- As soon as totality ends, you must either look away from the Sun or put your eclipse glasses back on.

Note: An alternative way to watch a partial (or annular) eclipse is by projecting an image of the Sun onto the ground or a screen with a "pinhole camera," which can be as simple as a small hole in a sheet of paper (as shown below). This also works with any household object with holes, such as a colander or sieve.

Eclipse glasses allow you to safely watch the partial phases of a solar eclipse.

That's when you'll see the brief diamond ring
Then the corona, a spectacular thing

This incredible image (also shown on the cover of this book) not only captures the totally eclipsed Sun but allows us to see features of the Moon as it blocks out the Sun's surface. Around the Moon, we see the pinkish chromosphere and the faint but beautiful light of the Sun's corona.

What's the corona?

With the start of totality, it's time to take off your eclipse glasses and look at the totally eclipsed Sun. The Sun's surface (photosphere) will now be completely hidden from view, allowing you to see the faint light of the Sun's atmosphere.

Astronomers divide the Sun's atmosphere into two main regions: a relatively thin layer called the *chromosphere*, which appears during totality as pinkish light very close to the Moon, and a *corona* that extends much farther from the Sun's surface. The word *corona* means "crown," because it looks like a crown around the eclipsed Sun.

Advanced Note: The corona consists of very thin (low density) but very hot gas that rises high above the Sun's surface. This gas is so hot that it gives off x-rays, which means astronomers can study the corona with x-ray telescopes. The intricate patterns and streamers that you see in the corona are shaped by the Sun's strong magnetic field. In case you are wondering how we stay safe from solar x-rays, it is because our atmosphere prevents them from reaching the ground — which is also why x-ray telescopes work only in space.

You'll look up in awe, to see stars in the day
Until (much too soon) the Moon's out of the way

This photo was taken during a total solar eclipse over the Great Wall of China (August 2008).

How dark will it get during totality?

The faint light of the corona gives the sky a twilight glow during totality. This means it won't be completely dark, but it should be dark enough for you to see bright planets (usually including Mercury, since it is always close to the Sun in the sky) and a few bright stars.

You'll also notice an interesting illusion: While the sky will darken gradually before totality, it will seem to brighten rather suddenly when totality ends. In reality, the lighting changes are the same before and after totality. The illusion occurs because your eyes have time to adapt as darkness approaches, but your eyes respond to the return of light from the Sun's surface as if someone just turned the lights on.

Advanced Note: While your eyes will see only a few bright stars, you can see many more with binoculars or a telescope. This fact helped scientists confirm Einstein's general theory of relativity, which is one of the most important theories in science. Einstein's theory predicts that the Sun's gravity should bend the light of distant stars, and scientists can test this prediction with careful measurements of the positions of stars during a total solar eclipse. Sure enough, the measurements agree with Einstein's predictions, a fact first verified during a total solar eclipse in 1919.

So be there with clear skies, and all is now set
For a breathtaking view you'll never forget.

This multiple exposure photograph shows the 2017 total solar eclipse from start to finish, with totality in the middle.

What should I pay attention to during totality?

The most important thing to do during your short time of totality is to enjoy the awe-inspiring experience. In general, this means it is much better to focus your attention on the sights and sounds around you than to spend a lot of time trying to take photos or doing anything else that will distract you.

We've already talked about many of the things you should watch for, including the diamond ring effect, the Sun's chromosphere and corona during totality, and stars and planets in the twilight glow of the sky. But there is much more. For example, near the times that the diamond ring effect appears, you can use binoculars with solar filters over the front lenses to see *Baily's beads*, in which tiny dots of sunlight shine through mountains and valleys along the edge of the Moon. You might also scan the horizon, noticing the sunset-like colors all around it. Keep in mind that no two eclipses are exactly the same, which is one reason why many people become "eclipse chasers," seeking to travel to every total solar eclipse that they can.

For more detail, including what to watch for if it is cloudy, and additional resources:
bigkidscience.com/eclipse/more

Glossary

annular eclipse A solar eclipse in which the Moon is relatively far from Earth as it passes in front of the Sun, so that it does not fully block the Sun, and we see a ring (or "annulus") of sunlight around the Moon. (p. 18)

Baily's beads Dots of sunlight that shine through openings among the mountains and valleys of the Moon, just before and after totality begins. (p. 27)

chromosphere The layer of the Sun's atmosphere that lies between the surface (photosphere) and the corona. (pp. 6, 25)

corona (of the Sun) The upper layer of the Sun's atmosphere that is generally visible only during a total solar eclipse. (pp. 6, 25)

diamond ring effect An effect that briefly makes the Sun look like a diamond ring as the last bits of sunlight disappear behind the Moon before totality, and again as sunlight first begins to reappear when totality ends. (p. 6)

eclipse glasses Specially made glasses that allow you to look at the Sun without damaging your eyes. (pp. 5, 24)

eclipse seasons Time periods (occurring about twice a year and lasting about 5 weeks each) during which eclipses occur, because the nodes of the Moon's orbit are lined up with the Sun and Earth. (p. 16)

ecliptic plane The plane defined by Earth's orbit around the Sun (represented by the pond surface in our "Moon pond" analogy). (p. 14)

full shadow (umbra) The region of an object's shadow in space in which sunlight is fully blocked. (p. 17)

lunar eclipse An event that occurs when Earth's shadow falls on the Moon, which can happen only when a full moon occurs near one of the nodes of the Moon's orbit. Lunar eclipses may be *total, partial,* or *penumbral.* (pp. 8, 15, 17)

nodes (of Moon's orbit) The two points where the Moon's orbit crosses through the ecliptic plane (the plane of Earth's orbit around the Sun). (p. 14)

partial shadow (penumbra) The region of an object's shadow in space in which sunlight is only partially blocked. (p. 17)

partial solar eclipse The solar eclipse you will see if you are located in the region of Earth touched by the Moon's partial shadow, so that your view of the Sun is only partially blocked. (p. 18)

path of totality For a total solar eclipse, this is the path on Earth along which it is possible to witness totality. (p. 7)

phases (of the Moon) The changing appearance of the Moon, from new to full and back again, that occurs as we view different portions of the Moon's sunlit and dark sides. The cycle of phases lasts about 29½ days (which is the origin of our word "month"; think "moonth"). (p. 13)

photosphere The visible surface of the Sun. (p. 6)

pinhole camera A very simple "camera" that projects an image through a small hole. For an eclipse, this can be as simple as a small hole in a sheet of paper or small holes in a household object (like a colander or sieve); openings between tree leaves may also act like pinhole cameras. (pp. 23, 24)

saros cycle The time period of about 18 years, 11 days, over which the general pattern of eclipses repeats. (pp. 7, 10)

science The search for knowledge that can be used to explain or predict natural phenomena in a way that can be confirmed through careful observations or experiments. (p. 9)

shadow bands Waves of light and dark that you may see rippling across the ground just before or after totality. (p. 23)

solar eclipse An event that occurs when the Moon's shadow falls on Earth, blocking light from the Sun, which can happen only when a new moon occurs near one of the nodes of the Moon's orbit. Solar eclipses may be *total*, *partial*, or *annular*. (pp. 8, 15, 18)

total solar eclipse The solar eclipse you will see if you are located in the region of Earth touched by the Moon's full shadow, so that your view of the Sun's surface is fully blocked and it becomes dark in the daytime. (p. 18)

totality For a solar eclipse, totality is the time during which the Sun is fully blocked by the Moon. For a lunar eclipse, totality is the time in which the entire Moon is engulfed in Earth's full shadow.

Suggested Activities

Modeling Solar Eclipses (Grades 3 and up)

Place a basketball or beachball on a table to represent the Sun. Find a smaller ball to represent the Moon, and your head will represent Earth. Stand a few steps from the table, holding the ball in your hand at arm's length.

- First, gradually rotate in place while holding the ball steady, so it goes around your head much as the Moon orbits Earth. Identify the positions that correspond to new moon and full moon. (*Hint*: See page 13.)
- Now, put the ball at the new moon position. Hold it still, cover one eye, and move your head until the ball completely blocks your view of the Sun ball on the table (you may need to hold your ball closer than arm's length for this to happen). What kind of eclipse does this represent? Explain.
- Move your head slightly in any direction until your Moon ball is only partly blocking the Sun ball. What kind of eclipse does this represent?
- Return the Moon ball (and your head) to the position at which it fully blocks the Sun ball, again with one eye covered. What should you do next to model an *annular* eclipse? Explain.

Modeling the Moon's Tilted Orbit (Grades 3 and up)

Start with the same setup as in the prior activity, but this time tape your Moon ball to a hula hoop, which will represent the Moon's orbit. Hold the hula hoop with your head (representing Earth) at the center. (It may be easier to have someone else hold the hula hoop for you.)

- Hold the hula hoop so that it is horizontal to the ground and sit or bend your knees until it is also level with the Sun ball on the table. The hula hoop now represents what the Moon's orbit would look like if it did not have any tilt compared to Earth's orbit around the Sun. With this orientation, when would you see eclipses?
- Now tilt the hula hoop so it is at an angle to the ground (with your head still in the middle), with the hula hoop higher than the Sun ball in front of you and lower than the Sun ball behind you. Is there still an eclipse at every new and full moon? Why or why not?
- Keep the hula hoop tilted the same way but walk slowly around the table until you find the places where eclipses are possible (as in the Moon pond model on page 16). How does this demonstration explain why we have lunar and solar eclipses about twice each year?

Eclipses to Scale (Grades 5 and up)

The prior activities were obviously not to scale. This activity explores why.

- Find a pinhead (or small ball bearing) that is about 1 millimeter in diameter to represent the Moon and a beachball (or large balloon) about 40 centimeters in diameter to represent the Sun. Note that these correctly represent the fact that the Sun's diameter is about 400 times that of the Moon.
- Place your "Sun" on a table in a large open field. Hold the pinhead at arm's length and walk away until, with one eye covered, you can completely block the view of your "Sun" with your pinhead. You now have a solar eclipse approximately to scale.
- How far away from your "Sun" are you? Based on this activity, explain why the prior activities — and most of the diagrams in this book — cannot easily be done to scale.

Eclipse Creativity (All Grade Levels)

This book offered one particular rhyme about a total solar eclipse experience. Come up with your own creative project to teach other people about eclipses. For example, you could write your own rhyme or rap, write a play, or create a poster, a piece of artwork, or a video. Be both creative and scientifically accurate.

Additional Activities

You'll find many more activities on the "Learn" screen of the *Totality* app and at www.BigKidScience.com/eclipse/classroom-activities.

Eclipse Science Summary

We've covered a lot of material in this book, so to help you consolidate your understanding, here is a brief summary of the major ideas.

1 There are two basic types of eclipse: solar and lunar.

A **solar eclipse** can occur only at new moon, when the Moon's shadow falls on Earth and blocks our view of the Sun.

A **lunar eclipse** can occur only at full moon, when Earth's shadow falls on the Moon.

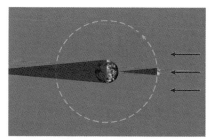
Solar eclipse

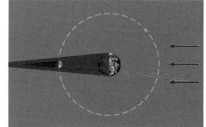
Lunar eclipse

2 We don't have eclipses at every new and full moon because the Moon's orbit around Earth is tilted compared to Earth's orbit around the Sun.

Eclipses occur only when a new or full moon happens near the points, called **nodes** (represented by the splashes in the Moon pond analogy), where the Moon's orbit crosses through Earth's orbital plane.

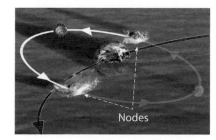
Nodes

3 As a result, there are about two time periods each year, called **eclipse seasons**, in which we'll see a solar eclipse at new moon and a lunar eclipse at full moon.

However, we don't have *exactly* two eclipse seasons each year. Instead, they come a little less than 6 months apart (about 173 days). As a result, the pattern of eclipses repeats over the time period called the **saros cycle**, which is about 18 years, 11 days.

4 The Sun's large size means that eclipse shadows have two distinct regions: a **full shadow** in which sunlight is fully blocked and a **partial shadow** in which sunlight is only partially blocked.

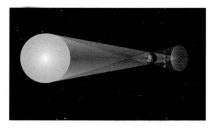

5 The shadow structure leads directly to the three types of lunar eclipse:

A **total lunar eclipse** occurs when Earth's full shadow engulfs the entire Moon.

A **partial lunar eclipse** occurs when only part of Earth's full shadow is on the Moon.

A **penumbral lunar eclipse** occurs when the Moon lies only in Earth's partial shadow.

Total lunar eclipse

Partial lunar eclipse

Penumbral lunar eclipse

6 Solar eclipses also come in three types, with one type arising primarily from the fact that the Moon's distance from Earth varies over its orbit:

A **total solar eclipse** occurs in the region of Earth touched by the Moon's full shadow.

A **partial solar eclipse** occurs in regions touched by the Moon's partial shadow.

An **annular eclipse** occurs when the Moon is relatively far from Earth in its orbit, so that its full shadow does not reach Earth, leaving a ring of sunlight around the Moon when it is directly in front of the Sun.

| Total solar eclipse | Partial solar eclipse | Annular solar eclipse |

7 While all eclipses are worth seeing, a total solar eclipse is much more spectacular than any other eclipse, because it is the only type of eclipse in which:

Day turns to night, allowing you to see planets and bright stars around the eclipsed Sun.

You'll be able to see the Sun's spectacular **corona**.

You'll get the full experience of the progression to totality, including changes in lighting, temperature, and animal behavior, plus the beautiful **diamond ring effect** just before totality begins (and when it ends).

Remember that you *can and should* remove your eclipse glasses during the brief period of totality, but don't look toward the Sun without them at any other time.

Warning: Except during totality, it is never safe to look directly at the Sun unless you are wearing your special eclipse glasses.

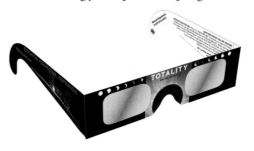

8 To experience totality, you must be located somewhere along the **path of totality** on eclipse day, with clear enough skies so that you can see the Sun. Use the *Totality* app to help you plan your eclipse trip.

9 Keep in mind that it is **science** that has made it possible for us to explain and predict eclipses, a fact that leads to a very important lesson: By focusing on science rather than fears or myths, we not only create understanding but also empower ourselves to build a more peaceful, fairer, and more sustainable future.

The full *Totality!* Rhyme

Also included